Jesse Owens

Jesse Owens, the world's greatest track-and-field athlete, clears yet another hurdle.

JUNIOR ▪ WORLD ▪ BIOGRAPHIES

Jesse Owens

RICK RENNERT

CHELSEA JUNIORS

a division of CHELSEA HOUSE PUBLISHERS

To my parents

Chelsea House Publishers
EDITOR-IN-CHIEF: Remmel Nunn
MANAGING EDITOR: Karyn Gullen Browne
COPY CHIEF: Juliann Barbato
PICTURE EDITOR: Adrian G. Allen
ART DIRECTOR: Maria Epes
DEPUTY COPY CHIEF: Mark Rifkin
ASSISTANT ART DIRECTOR: Noreen Romano
MANUFACTURING MANAGER: Gerald Levine
SYSTEMS MANAGER: Lindsey Ottman
PRODUCTION MANAGER: Joseph Romano
PRODUCTION COORDINATOR: Marie Claire Cebrián

JUNIOR WORLD BIOGRAPHIES

EDITOR: Remmel Nunn

Staff for JESSE OWENS
COPY EDITOR: Brian Sookram
PICTURE RESEARCHERS: Patricia Burns, Alan Gottlieb
SENIOR DESIGNER: Marjorie Zaum
COVER ILLUSTRATION: Alan Nahigian

First Printing

1 3 5 7 9 8 6 4 2

Library of Congress Cataloging-in-Publication Data
Rennert, Rick.
   Jesse Owens/Rick Rennert.
      p. cm.—(Junior world biographies)
   Summary: A biography of one of America's greatest track-and-field athletes,
the winner of four gold medals at the 1936 Olympic Games.
   ISBN 0-7910-1570-X
   1. Owens, Jesse, 1913–80—Juvenile literature. 2. Track-and-field
athletes—United States—Biography—Juvenile literature. [1. Owens, Jesse,
1913–80. 2. Track-and-field athletes. 3. Afro-Americans—Biography.]
I. Title. II. Series.
GV697.09R46 1992
796.42'092—dc20   90-21161
[B]   CIP
[92]   AC

Contents

The head of Nazi Germany, Adolf Hitler (standing in the car at left), leads the way to the opening ceremonies of the 1936 Olympic Games in Berlin.

1

August 2, 1936

For track-and-field star Jesse Owens, the dark clouds that hung over the bustling city of Berlin were a troubling sight. The 22-year-old American athlete had come to the capital of Germany to take part in the 1936 Summer Olympic Games. He planned to compete in 3 different events—the 100-meter dash, the 200-meter dash, and the long jump—and was eager to do well in all of them. But on the morning of his first race, the skies promised rain and threatened to dampen his high spirits.

While the clouds gathered over Berlin's Olympic Stadium, another kind of storm was threatening Europe. Adolf Hitler had established himself as the head of Germany three years earlier, and in that brief period of time he had turned his struggling nation into a mighty international power. But the man known as the Führer (German for "leader") was not ready to stop there. In fact, he had already begun to carry out his plans to rule the world.

Hitler hated anyone who was not white and of pure German stock. He held an even deeper hatred for people who were Jewish. Only a month after the Führer took office, he began to put Jews and other so-called enemies of the state into special detention centers known as concentration camps. He and his fellow members of the Nazi party would soon deal brutally with these people, killing millions of them in widespread acts of mass murder.

To help hide his evil intentions from the rest of the world, Hitler had won the right in 1933 to have Germany host the 1936 Olympic Games. His scheme was simple: He would invite the world's greatest athletes into his nation's capital and dare the foreign visitors to find anything wrong there.

Yet it was not enough for Hitler to merely sponsor the Olympic Games. He expected his German athletes to excel in each event. Their brilliant performances would prove to the entire world that the Aryans—people who were white, German-born, and non-Jewish—were "the master race" and that Germany was a land of supermen.

The first contest of the 1936 Olympics was the men's 100-meter run. It is regarded as the most exciting of all track events because the winner becomes known as "the world's fastest human." The Germans were counting on Erich Borchmeyer, their top sprinter, to finish in first place and win the gold medal. But he faced a mighty challenge in the person of Jesse Owens.

Just about everybody expected Owens to be the 1936 U.S. Olympic team's top performer—and with good reason. In 1935, when he was a second-year student at Ohio State University, he set five world records and tied another at a college track meet on May 25. Following that magnificent day, he trained hard for the next 14 months. He had to be in top form to earn a spot on the U.S. Olympic team, in part because he hoped to make the squad in not one but three different events.

Tryouts for the Olympics were held in New York City in mid-July 1936. By then, Owens had worked himself into the best shape of his life. He breezed through the trials and finished first in each of his two sprint events and the long jump.

Now people all across America could hardly wait for the Summer Games to begin. They were eager for Owens to show Germany's supermen that they were not really so super after all. But Owens knew that victory cannot be claimed until a race has been run and won. On July 13, two days before he departed for Berlin, he attended a huge dinner party in New York City along with his U.S. Olympic teammates. Seated next to Owens was the legendary baseball slugger Babe Ruth. The home-run king wasted no time in asking, "You gonna win at the Olympics, Jesse?"

"Gonna try," Owens replied.

"Everybody *tries*," Ruth said. "I succeed. Wanna know why?"

Owens nodded.

"Because I *know* I'm going to hit a home run just about every time I swing," Ruth said. "I'm surprised when I *don't*! And that isn't all there is to it. Because I know it, the pitchers, *they* know it, too."

Owens grinned at the baseball hero's great confidence in his own abilities. But the young Olympian did not fail to spot the good advice hidden in Ruth's remarks. It is not enough to *want* to win. You have to *know* that you will win.

Owens kept this piece of advice in mind

as he sailed on the SS *Manhattan*, the ocean liner that carried him across the Atlantic to Germany. "While I was going over on the boat," he recalled, "all I could think about was taking home one or two of those gold medals."

Owens continued to focus on winning the medals after he arrived in Europe on July 24. He refused to let anything distract him or destroy his confidence. As he walked through the streets of Berlin, he expected to be treated harshly because he was black. Instead, he was mobbed by admirers everywhere he went. Many Germans were true sports fans, and they wanted to get a close look at the brilliant young athlete who held so many world records.

The Berliners, in fact, did much more than look. Autograph seekers trailed Owens all over the training field, making it hard for him to practice. Photographers parked themselves outside his dormitory room window and snapped pictures of him. One morning, the noise of the clicking cameras was so loud that it woke him up.

*Jesse Owens (far right) battles the rain and cold on
August 2 as the 1936 Olympic Games begin. Seated
next to him are American sprinters Frank Wykoff (far
left) and Ralph Metcalfe (second from right) and
Swiss runner Paul Hänni.*

Jesse Owens springs into action on Berlin's Olympic Stadium track, displaying the form that made him America's top sprinter.

Owens, for his part, always treated these people very kindly. Sometimes he went so far as to say a few words to them in German. Yet he would let nothing disturb his concentration—not even when he discovered that the two new pairs of running shoes he had worn at the Olympic trials had been lost. He simply worked out in an old pair of spikes until new shoes could be found in a local sporting goods store.

By the time August 1 arrived, however, Owens was eager for the Games to begin. So were the more than 100,000 spectators who attended the opening ceremonies at Olympic Stadium. They greeted the arrival of Adolf Hitler with a loud roar. Next, they cheered the athletes from 52 nations who paraded around the track while military music blared over the loudspeakers.

Among the marchers were blacks, Jews, and people of other races and religions. None of them fit the Nazi model of a proper human being, least of all Jesse Owens. "We were everything Hitler hated," he said later. "But, in particular,

Hitler hated my skin. For I happened to have been the one who had set world records."

Owens put all the pomp and politics aside the following day, August 2. He had come to Germany to run and jump, and that was what he would do. Just before noon, he walked up to the starting line for the first elimination round of the men's 100-meter dash. He went through a few warm-ups, then dropped to his knees and, using a small silver shovel, began to dig a toehold to serve as his starting block.

Cold, drizzly rain was falling, making the cinder track slow and muddy. But just as he had dismissed the other distractions, Owens never gave the poor conditions a second thought. The only thing he focused on was running as fast as he could.

Owens shot out of his starting block the instant the starter fired his gun. He attained full speed in no time at all and burst toward the finish line. He reached it well ahead of his closest competitor, in a time of 10.3 seconds.

The crowd was stunned. In his very first race of the 1936 Olympics, Owens had not only come in first but had equaled his own world record. And he had done it under terrible running conditions. The German spectators responded by giving him the loudest ovation of his career. But as they, and Adolf Hitler, would soon find out, there was much more yet to come from Jesse Owens.

A teenage Jesse Owens during his high school days in Cleveland, Ohio.

2

"I Always Loved Running"

James Cleveland Owens grew up in a part of the world that was far removed from the busy cities of New York and Berlin. He was born on September 12, 1913, in Oakville, Alabama. "It was more dozens and dozens of farms," he said of his birthplace, "than a real town."

Nicknamed J.C., he was the youngest of Henry and Emma Owens's 10 children. A sharecropper, Henry farmed another man's property in exchange for a place to live and half the crops. The small wooden house was old and drafty, however, and J.C. often caught cold. To cure him, his mother would wrap cotton sacks around him. Then she would place him in front of the stove until he had sweated out his illness.

By the time J.C. was six years old, he had become strong enough to join his brothers and sisters on the nine-mile walk to school. His school was a one-room shack that Oakville's black population used on Sundays as a Baptist church.

J.C. would leave school whenever it was planting season or harvesttime to help his family work the fields. Life was hard for the Owenses. Even with so many of them to pitch in, they could never make much money. The worn-out land would simply not allow it. According to J.C., his father "had no more earthly possessions than [a] mule and the shredded clothes he wore to shield him from the sun."

J.C. and his family did not think of themselves as poor, though, because none of their neighbors were much better off. "We used to have a lot of fun," he said of his boyhood days. "We never had any problems. We always ate. The fact that we didn't have steak? Who had steak?"

J.C. liked to fish, swim, and play hide-and-seek in his free time. Best of all, he enjoyed running across the low hills of northern Alabama. "I wasn't very good at it," he recalled, "but I loved it because it was something you could do all by yourself, and under your own power. You could go in any direction, fast or slow as you wanted, fighting the wind if you felt like it, seeking out new sights just on the strength of your feet and the courage of your lungs."

One day, when J.C. was about nine years old, his mother told him to pack up his things. After he did that, he was to untie the mule that helped them plow the fields and haul their crops and take it to a neighbor's house. The family was going on a train that would take them far away, to a place where they would have no need for mules or other beasts of burden.

"Where's the train gonna take us, Momma?" J.C. wanted to know.

"It's gonna take us to a better life," she answered.

Like many other southern blacks, the Owenses were headed for America's industrial region, which they had heard was a worker's paradise. Lots of factories and plenty of job openings were to be found up North in states such as Illinois, Michigan, New York, and Ohio. J.C.'s sister Lillie had already moved to the city of Cleveland, Ohio, and had discovered that a person could make much more money there than on a sharecropper's farm.

The train that J.C. and his family boarded in Oakville also took them to Cleveland. There they settled in a small apartment in the city's black ghetto. It was, he admitted later, "a better world . . . most always" than the one they had known in Alabama.

Everyone in J.C.'s family found work in Cleveland. His father and brothers landed jobs in a nearby steel mill, and his mother and sisters cleaned houses and washed laundry. J.C. pitched in by taking a few part-time jobs. He worked in a shoemaker's shop, watered plants in a green-house, and served as a grocery store delivery boy. With the money they earned, they were able to buy new clothes and sturdy furniture—items that had been too costly for them in the South.

Life in Cleveland, J.C. quickly discovered, was nothing like what it had been in Oakville, where blacks and whites usually kept their dis-tance from one another. Just about every place in the big city, including his elementary school, was racially mixed. And, of course, everything was built on a much grander scale. The classes in his elementary school, for example, were not held in a one-room shack but in a large brick building.

People in the North also spoke with a dif-ferent type of accent. On J.C.'s first day at Bolton Elementary School, his teacher asked him what his name was.

The 10-year-old newcomer answered, "J.C. Owens," slurring the words together in his usual southern drawl. His accent caused the teacher to think he had said *Jesse* Owens.

"Jesse," she said out loud, wanting to make sure she had gotten it right.

J.C. was too timid to correct her, and so he was called Jesse from then on.

In spite of his initial shyness, Jesse made friends easily at school. When he was not working, he joined them in exploring his new neighborhood and found it to be a very exciting place. By the time he graduated from Bolton, he was no longer a country boy from Alabama but a streetwise teenager who knew the ins and outs of big-city life.

Jesse entered Fairmount Junior High School in 1927, when he was 14 years old. There, in the space of one week, he met two people who were to play a major part in his life.

The first person was a junior high student named Minnie Ruth Solomon. "I fell in love with her some the first time we ever talked," Jesse said, "and a little bit more every time after that." They began to date steadily following their first meeting

Jesse Owens works on the proper takeoff stance with his first track coach, Charles Riley.

and wound up getting married after they had graduated from high school.

The other person Jesse met was Charles Riley, a physical education teacher and Fairmount's track coach. "I'd noticed him watching me for a year or so," Jesse said of Riley, "especially when we'd play games where there was running or jumping."

One day, Riley called Jesse into his office and invited him to join the track team. The tall, thin youth leapt at the chance.

The first thing Riley did as Jesse's coach was to teach him to work patiently to obtain good results. "Train for four years from next Friday," Riley advised. He wanted Jesse to understand that it takes a while for young runners to reach their potential. Even so, Jesse began to think of himself as a runner in no time at all. "Days would pass," he later admitted, "when I didn't think of anything else."

Jesse trained only in the mornings because he held so many part-time jobs after school. "I got up with the sun," he recalled, "ate my breakfast even before my mother and sisters and brothers, and went to school, winter, spring, and fall alike to run and jump and bend my body this way and that for Mr. Charles Riley." They soon became so close that Jesse began to think of Riley as a second father. In fact, Jesse started calling him Pop.

After Jesse had worked out for several months, Pop Riley decided to clock him in the 100-yard dash. Jesse covered the distance in the amazingly speedy time of 11 seconds. Shocked by the reading on his stopwatch, the coach grabbed another one and asked Jesse to run the distance again. When he raced by once more in 11 seconds, Riley stood there in openmouthed astonishment. This youngster was even faster than either of them had ever imagined.

Jesse Owens (second from left) glides across the finish line to win a 100-meter dash in June 1932.

3

"To the Limit"

After several months of training, Jesse Owens finally suited up for the Fairmount Junior High School track team in the spring of 1928. He got off to a strong start in his first race, a quarter-mile run, and led most of the way. Then, just 50 yards from the finish line, 2 runners passed him. "I tried not to let it bother me, set my jaw hard, clenched my teeth, narrowed my eyes and gave all I had," he remembered. "Or I thought I gave all I had."

Pop Riley went over to Owens after the race and told him to stop pumping his arms and legs as he ran. He should run with a relaxed grace and keep his determination "all on the inside where no one can see it."

To make his point more clearly, Riley took Owens to a racetrack. The young sprinter saw at once that a horse was never stiff-legged as it galloped. Nor did its face ever change expression during a race.

"No horse has ever tried to stare another one down," Riley pointed out. "That's for actors."

This bit of advice led Owens to develop the fluid, effortless sprinting style that would soon amaze the sports world. But it was not the only reason for his success on the track. Owens also learned to guard against "the instinct to slack off, give in to the pain and give less than your best." He knew it was not enough to "wish to win through things falling right, or your opponents not doing their best." The secret to winning race after race, he said, was "going to the limit, past your limit, where victory is always found. Because it's victory over yourself."

Victory came often during Owens's first season on the track team. Along the way, he showed Coach Riley that he was not only a fast runner but a great leaper. He set the world record for junior high school students in both the long jump and the high jump.

Later in the year, Owens performed a different kind of leap: He jumped for joy. That happened when Riley introduced Jesse to his favorite track star, 1920 Olympic gold medalist Charlie Paddock. From then on, all the youngster could think about was reaching the Olympics, too. First, though, he had to go to high school.

In 1930, Owens enrolled at East Technical High School, which was only a few blocks from his home. Luckily for him, the school's track coach, Edgar Weil, allowed the young star to continue working with Charles Riley.

The hard workouts that Riley put Owens through continued to pay off. At track meet after track meet, Owens outran his competition and

Jesse Owens with (from left to right) his father, Henry; his mother, Emma; and Minnie Ruth Solomon, whom the star athlete married in 1935.

regularly saw his name appear in the local newspapers. Because he excelled at several events, one paper even called him a "one-man team."

By the summer of 1932, Owens was ready to become a member of a very special team. Although he was only a junior in high school, he had run well enough in the 100-yard and 220-yard dashes to qualify for a chance to make that year's U.S. Olympic squad. But 1932 was not to be Jesse Owens's year of glory. He lost both races to a powerful runner named Ralph Metcalfe and failed to land a spot on the team.

A few months later, after the Summer Games came to an end in Los Angeles, California, Owens managed to make up for his disappointing showing. He captured the 100-meter and 200-meter races in a meet that featured a group of touring Olympic athletes.

Now, with his senior year of high school about to begin, Owens was ready to shine. He started out by being named captain of the East Tech track team. (His classmates voted him student body president as well.) Then he posted an undefeated season to run his overall high school record to 75 victories in 79 races.

Owens capped off the 1933 track season in June, at the National Interscholastic Championship Meet in Chicago, Illinois. There he outdid even himself. He set a new world record (not just for high school athletes but for all athletes) in the 220-yard dash and equaled the world mark in the 100-yard dash. He also bettered his own long-jump record for schoolboys.

When word of these feats got back to Cleveland, everyone in his hometown realized that Jesse Owens was someone very special indeed. The mayor even went so far as to throw a parade for him through the city's streets. Seated alongside his parents in the back of a convertible, the celebrated athlete rode past a cheering crowd that lined the way to City Hall. Coach Riley followed in a car directly behind them.

Just 19 years old, Jesse tried hard to keep himself from thinking about all the fuss and attention. There was still plenty of work to be done. In addition to training for a spot on the U.S. Olympic team, he had to select a college to attend that fall.

Choosing a college was not an easy decision. Many universities throughout the country were eager to have Owens attend their school and run and jump for their track team. After much looking around, he decided on a college that was close to home: Ohio State University, in the state capital of Columbus.

As the autumn of 1933 drew near, Owens readied himself for an emotion-filled moment. It was time to say good-bye to Charles Riley and put his track career in the hands of another coach. Fortunately for the Ohio State freshman, the university's track coach was a young, ambitious man who treated Jesse as considerately as Riley had. His name was Larry Snyder.

Like all first-year students, Owens was not allowed to compete on a varsity team until his sophomore season. So he took part in freshman meets and, with Snyder's help, got rid of some bad habits. He worked to relax his upper body even more than before and to develop a more explosive takeoff at the start of a race. Owens learned to position himself at the starting line in a compact crouch so that he could uncoil more quickly into a full-speed run. And he made sure to get off to a fast start by improving his concentration as the starter was about to fire his pistol.

By 1935, when he joined Ohio State's varsity squad, Owens had already been training to run and jump for nearly eight years. In his first Big Ten Conference meet, he showed that he was ready to pick up right where he had left off in high school. He won 3 events and finished second in another, the 70-yard low hurdles.

As the season went on, Owens was beaten at a few other meets, most often by a strong, driving runner named Eulace Peacock. But those occasions were rare, and Jesse was overflowing with confidence by the time the Big Ten Championships were held on May 25, 1935, in Ann Arbor, Michigan.

Ohio State University track coach Larry Snyder helps Jesse Owens train for the high jump.

In front of 12,000 spectators, Owens put on the greatest single-day performance in the history of track and field. What made his showing all the more incredible was that he had hurt his back earlier in the week. The injury seemed to be so serious, in fact, that Coach Snyder wanted to keep him out of the Big Ten Championships. But Owens would have none of that. He wanted to compete. And did he ever.

To the amazement of everyone, Owens broke five world records and equaled another in a span of just 45 minutes. He began by tying the world record of 9.4 seconds in the 100-yard dash. Then he set new world marks in both the 220-yard dash and the 220-yard low hurdles. (After he had won these 220-yard events, he was also awarded the international record for each race at the slightly shorter distance of 200 meters.)

Last, but by no means least, came Owens's performance in the long jump. He prepared for it by jogging down the runway that led to the long-jump pit, counting out the number of steps he planned to take on his approach. He did this so he would make the jump with the same number of approach steps he always used in his training sessions—and to make sure that his very last step would be as close to the pit as possible. Anyone who stepped beyond the end of the takeoff board automatically had his jump disqualified by the officials.

His spirits boosted incredibly high by his earlier efforts in the day, an extremely confident Owens raced down the runway to begin his competition in the long jump. He leapt 26 feet, 3¼ inches. The distance shattered the old world mark.

Even if Owens had not been widely famous before this glorious day, he was certainly a celebrity now. In the weeks and months that followed, fans all across America paid careful attention to his every move. Track and field was a much more popular sport in the 1930s than it is today, and in one afternoon Jesse Owens had become its brightest star. He had proven that he was, in not just one but several events, the world's fastest human.

Jesse Owens warms up for the Summer Games by winning a 100-meter dash at the Penn Relays in April 1936.

4

On Track

It was not enough to be fast. Jesse Owens wanted to run in the 1936 Olympics, and for a chance for that to happen he had to be in the best shape of his life by the time of the tryouts. He knew as well as anyone that winning a sprint was not just a matter of speed. In going up against world-class runners, all of whom could fly down the track, the greatest challenge was to be able to squeeze out every last drop of effort. To get himself to go "to the limit"—especially in the last half of a race, when his body was already working as hard as it possibly could—required constant training and sheer willpower.

Owens had not yet reached peak form by the spring of 1936. Eulace Peacock, for one, had defeated him five times in six major races over the previous nine months. Jesse hoped to turn things around in late March, however, at an indoor track meet at Cleveland's Public Hall. Peacock was one of the runners entered in the 50-yard dash.

By racing against each other so often during the past couple of years, Owens and Peacock had established a good-natured rivalry. But when they got into their starting blocks for the finals of the 50-yard dash, they put their friendship aside and focused only on the race.

At the sound of the starter's gun, Owens exploded from his blocks and sped into the lead. Peacock was not so fortunate. His blocks slipped as he tried to bolt out of them, and that sent him stumbling. All he could do was watch helplessly while Owens easily defeated the other two finalists in the race.

When Owens discovered what had happened to Peacock, he immediately went over to his arch rival and told him that he wanted to run the race again. After some urging on Owens's part, Peacock finally agreed to a second race. The runners took a brief rest and then lined up once more. This time, the race went off without a hitch, and it ended with Peacock bursting across the finish line just inches ahead of Owens.

In spite of his friend's triumph, Jesse emerged from the event a double winner. He had captured the first race, and then his act of good sportsmanship had won over the crowd of 6,000. He had shown them that spirited competition is what sports is all about.

Thanks to Owens's recent string of defeats, some people thought Peacock was the most likely sprinter to land a spot on the U.S. Olympic team. But Owens, well aware that an athlete's performance goes through periods of peaks and valleys, knew better. His goal was to be at his best not in March or April but in July and August, in time for both the Olympic trials and the Games.

The first sign that Owens was on schedule came on May 16, 1936, less than a month before the start of the Olympic trials in New York City. At a meet in Madison, Wisconsin, the college junior broke the world record in the 100-yard dash with a time of 9.3 seconds. He followed that up a week later with another eye-opening performance at the Big Ten Championships, when he won all four of his events.

Peacock failed to keep pace with Owens's successes. One month after his victory at Cleveland's Public Hall, Peacock severely pulled a thigh muscle during a race at the Penn Relays. He tried hard to recover from the injury in the 10 weeks that followed, but his leg did not get much better, and he finished out of the running at the Olympic trials.

Owens ran into no such problems. He finished first at the trials in the 100-meter and 200-

Sprinter Eulace Peacock (right) was Jesse Owens's chief rival as well as his good friend.

meter dashes and the long jump. At long last, the final hurdles to his boyhood dream had been cleared. After countless hours of training and practice, he was going to the Olympics.

In July, 22-year-old Jesse Owens left for Germany on the luxury liner SS *Manhattan*. During his week-long voyage across the Atlantic Ocean, he kept pretty much to himself. He left the champagne and rich food to others. He was not about to risk throwing away everything he had worked for before he even stepped on German soil.

Nor would Owens let himself be affected by all the excitement he seemed to cause among the German people. "I wasn't in Berlin to compete against any one athlete," he said later on. "The purpose of the Olympics, anyway, was to do your best. As I'd learned long ago from Charles Riley, the only victory that counts is the one over yourself."

Owens began his march to victory by winning the first two elimination rounds of the men's 100 meters on August 2. He returned to Olympic Stadium the following afternoon for the semifinals and finals of the 100-meter race. Two brief rain showers at lunchtime had muddied the track, making for poor running conditions once again. But Owens had come too far and had worked too hard to be troubled by the cold, damp weather. He easily won his semifinal race, in 10.4 seconds. Then he put on his sweat suit and wrapped himself in a heavy blanket to await the start of the finals at 5:00 P.M.

Adolf Hitler arrived at the stadium shortly before the race began. Greeted by a torrent of cheers, he quickly took a seat in the box of honor. He did not want to miss a single moment of the event he expected to witness: Erich Borchmeyer's gold-medal victory over Jesse Owens.

Owens paid no notice to the German leader. "When I lined up in my lane for the finals of the 100 meters," he recalled, "I was looking only at the finish line. . . . Five of the world's fastest humans wanted to beat me to it."

The crowd grew eerily silent as the starter approached the track and raised his right hand to fire the starter's pistol. Then the gun gave a mighty crack, and everyone in the stadium followed instantly with a tremendous roar. The race was under way, with all six men bunched together on the wet cinders. "To a sprinter," Owens said later on, "the hundred-yard dash is over in *three* seconds, not nine or ten. The first 'second' is when you come out of the blocks. The next is when you look up and take your first few strides to attain gain position. By that time the race is actually about half over.

"The final 'second'—the longest slice of

Jesse Owens wins his second Olympic gold medal by running ahead of the pack in the 200-meter dash.

time in the world for an athlete—is that last half of the race, when you really bear down and see what you're made of. It seems to take an eternity, yet is all over before you can think what's happening."

It was during the "final second" that Owens surged ahead of the rest of the field. He flew down lane 1 and reached the finish line several strides ahead of fellow American Ralph Metcalfe.

Owens was clocked at 10.3 seconds, which equaled both his Olympic and world marks.

"Yesseh Oh-vens! Yesseh Oh-vens!" The crowd roared its approval as Owens took his victory lap around the stadium. When he went to the winner's stand to receive his gold medal and be saluted by 100,000 spectators, he was overcome with emotion.

"My eyes blurred," he remembered, "as I heard the Star-Spangled Banner played, first faintly and then loudly, and then saw the American flag slowly raised for my victory." It was, he said without hesitation, the happiest moment of his career.

Jesse Owens soars through the air during the long-jump competition at the 1936 Olympics.

CHAPTER

5

"I Wasn't Going to Come Down"

When Jesse Owens was perched atop the victory stand after winning the 100-meter dash in the 1936 Olympics, he turned to face Adolf Hitler in the Führer's viewing box. Both men were surrounded by the spectacle of the awards ceremony: a stadium filled with cheering fans, a German band playing "The Star-Spangled Banner," and the U.S. flag flying in honor of the American sprinter's gold-medal–winning performance. Owens bowed to Hitler, who returned a stiff salute and then looked away.

"The Americans should be ashamed of themselves, letting Negroes win their medals for them," the Führer said.

"He is an American citizen," one of Hitler's aides pointed out, "and it's not for us to decide whom the Americans let compete. Besides, he's a friendly and educated man, a college student." In fact, the aide suggested, rather than ignore the athlete, Owens should be invited to visit the Führer in his box.

"Do you really think," Hitler yelled angrily, "I will allow myself to be photographed shaking hands with a Negro?"

Adolf Hitler did not become any happier the following day, when Owens captured his second gold medal by smashing the world record in the 200-meter dash. After watching the black American speed across the wet track in 20.7 seconds, the German leader hurried out of the stadium before the awards ceremony began. He did not want to see Owens receive another medal.

Nazi Germany now had just one hope left. Only one of their athletes still had a chance to put Jesse Owens in his place: Luz Long, Germany's long-jump champion.

Tall, sandy-haired, and blue-eyed, Long was "a supreme example of Aryan perfection," said Owens. The first time they stood near each other on the field, Jesse saw "a perfectly proportioned body . . . honed by tens of thousands of obvious hours of sweat and determination. He may have been my arch enemy, but I had to stand there in awe and just stare at Luz Long for several seconds."

To reach the finals of the long-jump competition, each person was given three chances to leap at least 23 feet, 5 inches. Long topped that distance with such ease in his first attempt that he was laughing as he climbed out of the long-jump pit.

Owens, whose year-old mark of 26 feet,

3¼ inches was still the world record, should have found it just as easy to qualify for the final round. But he did not.

Still wearing his sweat suit, Owens loosened up for his first jump by jogging down the runway to measure his approach steps. As soon as he reached the long-jump pit, however, he stopped in his tracks. To Jesse's utter amazement, he saw a nearby official raise a red flag to signal that the run-through would be counted as an unsuccessful attempt. Apparently, practice runs were not allowed in Olympic competition.

Owens immediately tried to relax himself. He knew he had to put every bit of effort into his next attempt. But in his eagerness to qualify for the finals, he stepped past the takeoff board in his second leap. Once again, the official raised a red flag to signal that Owens had not made a successful jump.

Now, with only one leap left, Jesse was in a state of shock. "Panic," he recalled, "crept into my body, taking me over." He put on his sweatshirt and tried to gather his thoughts in what he later said was the most nerve-racking moment of his career.

Just then, Luz Long walked over to Owens, put his hand on Jesse's shoulder, and asked, "What has taken your goat, Jazze Owens?" Even a nervous Owens could not help but smile at those funny-sounding words.

Long then made a clever suggestion. He knew Owens would not take it easy on his next leap; Jesse was someone who always performed all out. And yet, if Owens put everything he had into the jump, he might commit another foul. So Long laid down a towel six inches in front of the

Germany's Luz Long makes his final leap in the long-jump competition.

takeoff board and told Owens to begin his leap at the towel. That way, he would be able to give 100 percent while not stepping beyond the board.

Owens sped down the runway and began his jump right at the towel. He sailed into the air and landed at a spot that was 25 feet, 9¾ inches from the takeoff board. The leap set a new Olympic record. But more important to Jesse, it put him in the finals.

With none of the four other finalists a serious threat to finish in first place, the stage was now set for a spectacular duel between Long and Owens for the gold medal.

Long began the battle. Soaring through the air with his hands thrown high above his head, he matched the old Olympic record with his first leap.

Long did even better on his second attempt. Urged on by a roaring crowd, he equaled the new Olympic mark that Owens had set earlier in the day. Jesse was the first person to rush over to Long and hug him in a show of congratulations.

But Owens, who had fouled in his first attempt, was not about to be outdone. When it was again his turn to jump, he stood perfectly still at the start of the runway. Then he leaned slightly forward and sprinted to the takeoff board. At the end of his approach, he vaulted into the air, hitch-kicked his legs in midflight, and landed 26 feet, ½ inch from the board—nearly 3 inches farther than Long's best effort. The leap put Owens in front in their competition for the gold medal.

Long now had only one chance left to regain the lead. As he positioned himself at the head of the runway, the 100,000 spectators grew so quiet that the many flags in the stadium could be heard slapping against their poles. Everyone knew that Luz Long needed a record-breaking jump to top Owens's last leap.

Like Owens had in the elimination round, Long now put everything he had into his last jump of the competition. But in his attempt to come up with a superhuman effort, he stepped over the front edge of the takeoff board. His jump was disallowed.

Groans echoed throughout the stadium. Jesse Owens had won the gold medal over Luz Long.

Owens still had one jump left, however, and he managed to give the fans one last treat. "I decided I wasn't going to come down," he said of his final leap in the long-jump competition. "I was going to fly. I was going to stay up in the air forever." He very nearly did. Owens sailed to an Olympic and world record leap of 26 feet, 5¼ inches, a mark that would stand for another 24 years.

Long was the first to congratulate Owens on his remarkable feat. The German high jumper ran over to Jesse, grabbed his left hand, and raised

To most people, the spirited competition between Luz Long and Jesse Owens in the long jump was the high point of the 1936 Olympics.

it triumphantly in the air, in full view of Adolf Hitler. With the crowd shouting, "Yesseh Oh-vens! Yesseh Oh-vens!" the two athletes walked off the field arm in arm.

By nightfall, Owens and Long had become inseparable. They spent several hours talking as best they could, in spite of their language differences. They were the same age, 22, and both had come from poor families. They loved to play sports and had begun to worry what their futures would be like when the Olympics were over. They also discussed the terrible problems of racial prejudice in Germany and the United States.

As the two star athletes sealed their new-found friendship, newspapers around the world reported the story. The most memorable part of the 1936 Olympics, the papers said, was not the grand show put on by Adolf Hitler's "master race," nor was it the gold-medal victories by a black American sprinter. It was the special relationship forged by Jesse Owens and Luz Long, so-called enemies who had worked together to discover the best within themselves.

Jesse Owens displays the gold medals he received for winning the 100-meter and 200-meter dashes and the high jump. He earned a fourth gold medal by running the first part of the 400-meter relay for the U.S. team.

6

A Hero's Welcome

For Jesse Owens, the competition was over. He had entered three different events and had won a gold medal in each one. He could now sit back and root for his American teammates.

There was just one sprint event left in the 1936 Olympics, the 400-meter relay race. The Americans had put together quite a promising relay team even without Owens. It consisted of three world-class runners, Foy Draper, Marty Glickman, and Sam Stoller—each of whom was looking forward to his first taste of action in the Summer Games—as well as veteran Frank Wykoff, who would be running the all-important final leg.

But on August 7, the day before the relays were to begin, Owens suddenly found himself in the middle of an ugly situation. U.S. track coach Lawson Robertson told him that both he and Ralph Metcalfe were going to run in the 400-meter relay. The two sprinters they would be replacing were the American team's only Jewish members—Glickman and Stoller.

According to Robertson, the Germans had been saving their best sprinters for the relays. If Owens were to run the first 100 meters and Metcalfe were to follow him in the second leg, the American team would have a much better shot at emerging with a victory.

Owens tried to stick up for the two teammates Robertson wanted to cast aside. "Coach, let Sam and Marty run," Jesse argued. "I've had enough. I've won three gold medals. Let them run, they deserve it."

But Owens's words fell on deaf ears. Glickman and Stoller would become the only two U.S. Olympic team members who did not get a chance to compete at the 1936 Summer Games. They were dropped from the race, the two sprinters said, not because the Germans had put together a "super" squad but because the heads of the U.S. team did not want to see any Jews run in Berlin.

On the morning of August 8, Owens realized that the matter was beyond his control and agreed to run the relay. First up was the elimination round, in which the Germans proved they were not a serious threat to capture the gold medal. Owens, meanwhile, ran the first 100 meters and paced America's four-man squad to a world-record-tying time.

The Americans ran even faster in the finals that afternoon. Owens shot out to a comfortable lead and then saw Metcalfe, Draper, and Wykoff lengthen the margin. By the end of the 400-meter

A conquering hero: Jesse Owens (at back of lead car) is cheered by his hometown fans in Cleveland shortly after returning from Berlin. He was the first person ever to win four gold medals in Olympic competition.

race, they had set a new world record of 39.8 seconds.

Thanks to his team's victory, Jesse Owens had captured his fourth gold medal. It was a record number for a track-and-field athlete. Just as amazing, he had broken the Olympic mark in each of the four events he had entered.

Coach Larry Snyder came to Owens's dormitory room later that evening to discuss Jesse's plans for the future. The college junior could complete his degree, Snyder explained, or he could drop out of school to make some money from his newfound celebrity.

"I'm anxious to finish my college career," the most famous athlete in the world told a reporter the next morning, "but I can't afford to miss this chance if it really means big money. I can always go back and get a degree."

Great things certainly appeared to be in store for Owens upon his return to the United States. He received a hero's welcome everywhere he went. The cities of New York, Cleveland, and

Columbus each treated him to a victory parade. Show-business agents offered him fantastic money-making deals. Entertainers wanted to take him on tour. Movie studios talked about filming his life's story.

Then, bit by bit, everything turned sour. Owens had been home for little more than a week when he signed a contract to work with a booking agent named Marty Forkins. Jesse was subsequently told by the Amateur Athletic Union, which governed amateur sports in America, that, by signing the contract he had become a professional athlete and could not compete in college track meets ever again. On top of that news, all the deals that Owens had been promised began to fall through.

"After I came home from the 1936 Olympics with my four medals," the conquering hero said, "it became increasingly apparent that everyone was going to slap me on the back, want to shake my hand or have me up to their suite. But no one was going to offer me a job."

Jesse Owens returned to Ohio State University at the age of 27 to serve as an assistant track coach and to earn his college degree.

7

The Fastest
Man in
the World

Instead of finding instant commercial success after the 1936 Olympics, Jesse Owens had to scramble to earn a living. It took a lot of time and energy, but he managed to cash in on his worldwide fame. He spoke at banquets, endorsed clothing, and accepted any other worthwhile offer dug up by his business agent, Marty Forkins.

In late 1936, Owens agreed to compete in a match race against Cuba's fastest sprinter, Conrado Rodriques. Jesse arrived in the Caribbean nation on Christmas Day, only to learn that Rodriques was no longer willing to go through with the race. The Cuban runner feared he would lose his amateur standing by competing against a professional.

Undeterred, Forkins arranged for his client to run against a thoroughbred racehorse at half-time of a soccer game. Owens said it did not escape his notice that he had "toppled from the Olympic heights to make my living competing with animals" in just a matter of months. He went through with the race, though, and beat the horse by several yards.

A few weeks later, Owens finally landed a huge money-making deal. Bill "Bojangles" Robinson, one of America's best-known black entertainers, had told the track star while he was coming home from Berlin, "Don't do anything till you see me!" In January 1937, Robinson arranged for Owens to be hired as the bandleader of a 12-piece orchestra. The job paid $100,000, a very large amount in those days, and lasted for several months.

Owens then formed a hotshot basketball squad that put on exhibition games across America, and he started a traveling softball team. He held running demonstrations in which he competed against the likes of heavyweight boxing champion Joe Louis and professional baseball players. He worked as a bathhouse attendant and a playground director. And he opened his own business, the Jesse Owens Dry Cleaning Company, in Cleveland.

Owens tried all different kinds of work, but nothing left him completely satisfied. He could run faster and jump farther than anyone alive, yet those talents were not enough to get him a good, steady job. In 1940, it was impossible for an athlete—even one as gifted as Jesse Owens—to make a living on the track-and-field circuit.

When Owens turned 27 years old, he decided to go back to Ohio State. He hoped that by getting his degree and starting a new career he would not have to seek out business ventures that took him far away from his family. By this time, Jesse and his wife, Ruth, had three young daughters: Gloria, Marlene, and Beverly. In the fall of 1940, they all moved to Columbus.

Owens paid for his schooling by helping Larry Snyder coach the track team. Jesse, however, had never been the best student, and now, with a growing family to support, he did not find it any easier to sit down and study. To make matters worse, he had to take the tough courses he had avoided during his first three years of college.

Halfway through his second year back at Ohio State, Owens realized he would never graduate. His grades were simply not high enough. He left school and accepted a post as head of a national physical fitness organization. A year later, he took a job as personnel officer for the Ford Motor Company.

But at the end of 1945, Owens returned to his old barnstorming ways. "I'd found that I could get more done with no regular job or regular hours at all," he said, "but by being on my own, flying to speak here, help with a public relations campaign for some client there, tape my regular jazz radio show one morning at 5:00 A.M. before leaving on a plane for another city or another continent three hours later to preside over a major sporting event." Owens added that "people who worked with me or knew me still called me the 'world's fastest human' because I almost never stopped."

Owens eventually saw all his hard work pay off. In 1950, a year when the hottest new invention in America was the television set, he was named the greatest track-and-field athlete in history. Business leaders, looking for someone to promote their products on TV, suddenly realized that Jesse Owens was their man. He was a national hero, the first person in the United States to put Adolf Hitler in his place. But he was also an honest and hard worker who perfectly symbolized the American way of life.

Owens became so swamped with business offers that he formed his own public relations company to keep track of them all. While he was following a busy schedule of publicity appearances, the U.S. government asked him to travel overseas as an international ambassador of goodwill. Then the state of Illinois appointed him chairman of two different programs to promote sports activities for poor youths. He was running in different directions all over again.

Owens did not slow down from this hectic pace for the next 25 years—not until he reached the age of 65, when he finally listened to Ruth's constant pleading that he retire to a quieter life. They settled in Scottsdale, Arizona, in 1978.

The following year, doctors discovered that Owens had lung cancer. He died of the disease on March 31, 1980, at a hospital in Tucson, Arizona.

Owens received many honors in the years that followed. Athletic awards and annual track meets were named after him. The street leading to Olympic Stadium in Berlin was renamed Jesse Owens Strasse. During the opening ceremonies of the 1984 Summer Games, his granddaughter Gina

Jesse Owens finally received a college degree in 1972, when Ohio State University awarded him an honorary doctor of athletic arts degree.

Hemphill was asked to carry the Olympic torch, which is used to light a huge fire bowl at the start of each of the Olympic Games.

All of these honors emphasized a point once made by the poor Alabama sharecropper's son who had driven himself to the height of success. "In America," Jesse Owens said, "anyone can become somebody. Does that sound corny in this day and age? Well, it happened to me, and I believe it can happen to anybody in one way or another."

Chronology

September 12, 1913	James Cleveland Owens born in Oakville, Alabama
ca. 1922	Moves to Cleveland, Ohio
1927	Enrolls at Fairmount Junior High School; meets Coach Charles Riley
1930	Enrolls at East Technical High School
1933	Ties the world record in the 100-yard dash and breaks the world record in the 220-yard dash at the National Interscholastic Championship Meet; enrolls at Ohio State University
1935	Breaks five world records and ties a sixth at the Big Ten Championships; marries Minnie Ruth Solomon
1936	Breaks the world record in the 100-yard dash; earns a place on the U.S. Olympic team; wins Olympic gold medals in the 100 meters, 200 meters,

long jump, and 400-meter
relay; signs agency contract;
loses amateur status

1937   Becomes a bandleader and the
        owner of a basketball team and
        dry-cleaning company

1940   Re-enrolls at Ohio State
        University

1941   Leaves school; takes job as
        head of the Civilian Defense
        Office's national fitness
        program

1942   Takes job as personnel officer
        for the Ford Motor Company

1950   Named the greatest track-and-
        field athlete in history by the
        Associated Press; travels as a
        goodwill ambassador for the
        State Department; appointed
        head of Illinois' Athletic
        Commission and Youth
        Commission

1960   Forms a public relations
        company

1978   Retires to Scottsdale, Arizona

March 31, 1980   Dies of lung cancer in Tucson,
                  Arizona

Glossary

ambassador an official representative of a government

Aryan those people who are white, German-born, and non-Jewish

cinder track a running track with a surface made of ash

concentration camp a place where political prisoners are confined

führer the German word for leader

Nazi party (National Socialist German Workers' party) political party that ruled Germany under Adolf Hitler from 1933 to 1945; its beliefs were based on racial hatred and devotion to the führer

Olympic Games a series of international amateur sports contests held every four years and modeled on sports competitions held in ancient Greece

personnel officer   a person involved in the hiring of new workers and in the relationship of workers with their employers

public relations   activities that are designed to create public interest in a person, product, idea, business, or institution

sharecropper   a person who farms another person's land in exchange for a place to live and half the crops

starting block   a device made of two blocks mounted on either side of a frame which is anchored to the ground to provide a runner with a hard surface against which to brace his or her feet at the beginning of a race

track and field   competitive sports, such as foot racing, hurdling, jumping, vaulting, and weight throwing, that are performed on a running track and on the adjacent field

Picture Credits

Rick Rennert is a Haverford College graduate who works as a book editor in New York City. He loves to run and has raced in several marathons, although at not quite the world-record pace of a Jesse Owens.